This book belongs to

_____

_____

_____

_____

SHAKESPEARE'S

SHAKESPEARE'S

LOVE SONNETS

Poetry by
WILLIAM SHAKESPEARE

Illustrations by
CAITLIN KEEGAN

CHRONICLE BOOKS
SAN FRANCISCO

hall I compare thee to a summer's day?
Thou art more lovely and more temperate:
Rough winds do shake the darling buds of May,
And summer's lease hath all too short a date:
Sometime too hot the eye of heaven shines,
And often is his gold complexion dimm'd;
And every fair from fair sometime declines,
By chance or nature's changing course untrimm'd;
But thy eternal summer shall not fade
Nor lose possession of that fair thou ow'st;
Nor shall death brag thou wander'st in his shade,
When in eternal lines to time thou grow'st:
So long as men can breathe or eyes can see,
So long lives this, and this gives life to thee.

evouring Time, blunt thou the lion's paws,

And make the earth devour her own sweet brood;

Pluck the keen teeth from the fierce tiger's jaws,

And burn the long-liv'd phoenix in her blood;

Make glad and sorry seasons as thou fleets,

And do whate'er thou wilt, swift-footed Time,

To the wide world and all her fading sweets;

But I forbid thee one most heinous crime:

O! carve not with thy hours my love's fair brow,

Nor draw no lines there with thine antique pen;

Him in thy course untainted do allow

For beauty's pattern to succeeding men.

Yet, do thy worst, old Time: despite thy wrong,

My love shall in my verse ever live young.

As an unperfect actor on the stage,

Who with his fear is put besides his part,

Or some fierce thing replete with too much rage,

Whose strength's abundance weakens his own heart;

So I, for fear of trust, forget to say

The perfect ceremony of love's rite,

And in mine own love's strength seem to decay,

O'ercharg'd with burthen of mine own love's might.

O! let my looks be then the eloquence

And dumb presagers of my speaking breast,

Who plead for love and look for recompense

More than that tongue that more hath more express'd.

O! learn to read what silent love hath writ:

To hear with eyes belongs to love's fine wit.

hen, in disgrace with fortune and men's eyes,

    I all alone beweep my outcast state,

        And trouble deaf heaven with my bootless cries,

And look upon myself and curse my fate,

Wishing me like to one more rich in hope,

Featured like him, like him with friends possess'd,

Desiring this man's art, and that man's scope,

With what I most enjoy contented least;

Yet in these thoughts myself almost despising,

Haply I think on thee, and then my state,

Like to the lark at break of day arising

From sullen earth, sings hymns at heaven's gate;

For thy sweet love remember'd such wealth brings

That then I scorn to change my state with kings.

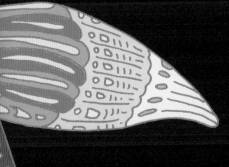

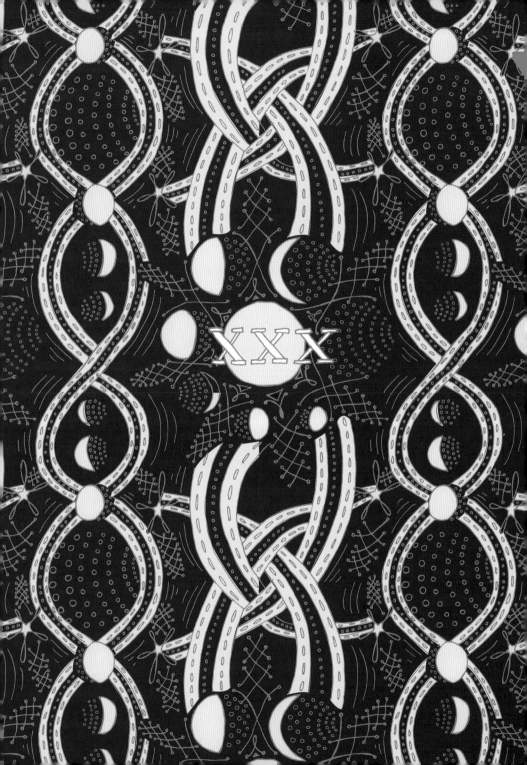

XXX

When to the sessions of sweet silent thought

I summon up remembrance of things past,

I sigh the lack of many a thing I sought,

And with old woes new wail my dear time's waste:

Then can I drown an eye, unused to flow,

For precious friends hid in death's dateless night,

And weep afresh love's long since cancell'd woe,

And moan the expense of many a vanish'd sight:

Then can I grieve at grievances foregone,

And heavily from woe to woe tell o'er

The sad account of fore-bemoaned moan,

Which I new pay as if not paid before.

But if the while I think on thee, dear friend,

All losses are restor'd and sorrows end.

XXXIII

Full many a glorious morning have I seen
Flatter the mountain-tops with sovereign eye,
Kissing with golden face the meadows green,
Gilding pale streams with heavenly alchemy;
Anon permit the basest clouds to ride
With ugly rack on his celestial face,
And from the forlorn world his visage hide,
Stealing unseen to west with this disgrace:
Even so my sun one early morn did shine
With all triumphant splendor on my brow;
But out! alack! he was but one hour mine,
The region cloud hath mask'd him from me now.
Yet him for this my love no whit disdaineth;
Suns of the world may stain when heaven's sun staineth.

What is your substance, whereof are you made,

That millions of strange shadows on you tend?
Since every one, hath every one, one shade,
And you but one, can every shadow lend.
Describe Adonis, and the counterfeit
Is poorly imitated after you;
On Helen's cheek all art of beauty set,
And you in Grecian tires are painted new:
Speak of the spring and foison of the year,
The one doth shadow of your beauty show,
The other as your bounty doth appear;
And you in every blessed shape we know.
In all external grace you have some part,
But you like none, none you, for constant heart.

Not marble, nor the gilded monuments

Of princes, shall outlive this powerful rhyme;

But you shall shine more bright in these contents

Than unswept stone besmear'd with sluttish time.

When wasteful war shall statues overturn,

And broils root out the work of masonry,

Nor Mars his sword nor war's quick fire shall burn

The living record of your memory.

'Gainst death and all-oblivious enmity

Shall you pace forth; your praise shall still find room

Even in the eyes of all posterity

That wear this world out to the ending doom.

So, till the judgment that yourself arise,

You live in this, and dwell in lovers' eyes.

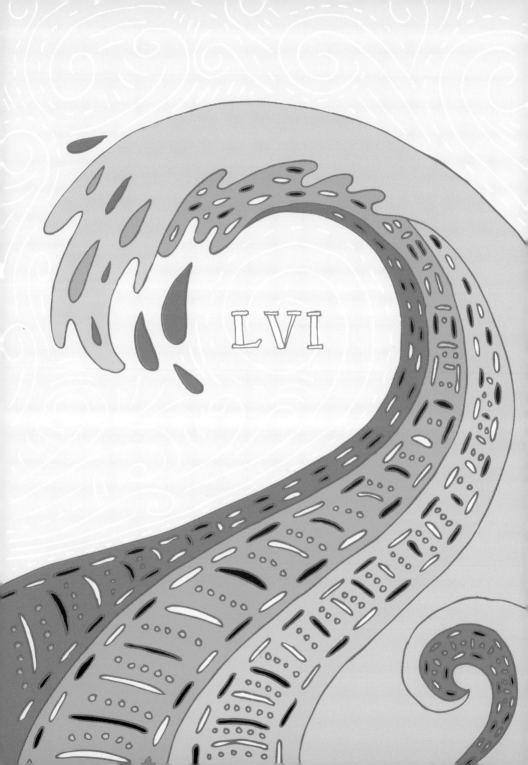

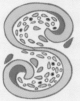weet love, renew thy force; be it not said

Thy edge should blunter be than appetite,

Which but to-day by feeding is allay'd,

To-morrow sharpened in his former might:

So, love, be thou, although to-day thou fill

Thy hungry eyes even till they wink with fulness,

To-morrow see again, and do not kill

The spirit of love with a perpetual dulness.

Let this sad interim like the ocean be

Which parts the shore, where two contracted new

Come daily to the banks, that when they see

Return of love, more blest may be the view;

Else call it winter, which being full of care,

Makes summer's welcome thrice more wished, more rare.

Being your slave what should I do but tend,

Upon the hours, and times of your desire?
I have no precious time at all to spend;
Nor services to do, till you require.
Nor dare I chide the world-without-end hour,
Whilst I, my sovereign, watch the clock for you,
Nor think the bitterness of absence sour,
When you have bid your servant once adieu;
Nor dare I question with my jealous thought
Where you may be, or your affairs suppose,
But, like a sad slave, stay and think of naught
Save, where you are, how happy you make those.
So true a fool is love, that in your will,
Though you do any thing, he thinks no ill.

LX

Like as the waves make towards the pebbled shore,

So do our minutes hasten to their end;

Each changing place with that which goes before,

In sequent toil all forwards do contend.

Nativity, once in the main of light,

Crawls to maturity, wherewith being crown'd,

Crooked elipses 'gainst his glory fight,

And Time that gave doth now his gift confound.

Time doth transfix the flourish set on youth

And delves the parallels in beauty's brow,

Feeds on the rarities of nature's truth,

And nothing stands but for his scythe to mow:

And yet to times in hope, my verse shall stand,

Praising thy worth, despite his cruel hand.

ince brass, nor stone, nor earth, nor boundless sea,

But sad mortality o'ersways their power,

How with this rage shall beauty hold a plea,

Whose action is no stronger than a flower?

O! how shall summer's honey breath hold out,

Against the wrackful siege of battering days,

When rocks impregnable are not so stout,

Nor gates of steel so strong but Time decays?

O fearful meditation! where, alack,

Shall Time's best jewel from Time's chest lie hid?

Or what strong hand can hold his swift foot back?

Or who his spoil of beauty can forbid?

O! none, unless this miracle have might,

That in black ink my love may still shine bright.

LXXI

o longer mourn for me when I am dead

Than you shall hear the surly sullen bell

Give warning to the world that I am fled

From this vile world with vilest worms to dwell:

Nay, if you read this line, remember not

The hand that writ it, for I love you so

That I in your sweet thoughts would be forgot,

If thinking on me then should make you woe.

O! if, I say you look upon this verse,

When I perhaps compounded am with clay,

Do not so much as my poor name rehearse;

But let your love even with my life decay;

Lest the wise world should look into your moan

And mock you with me after I am gone.

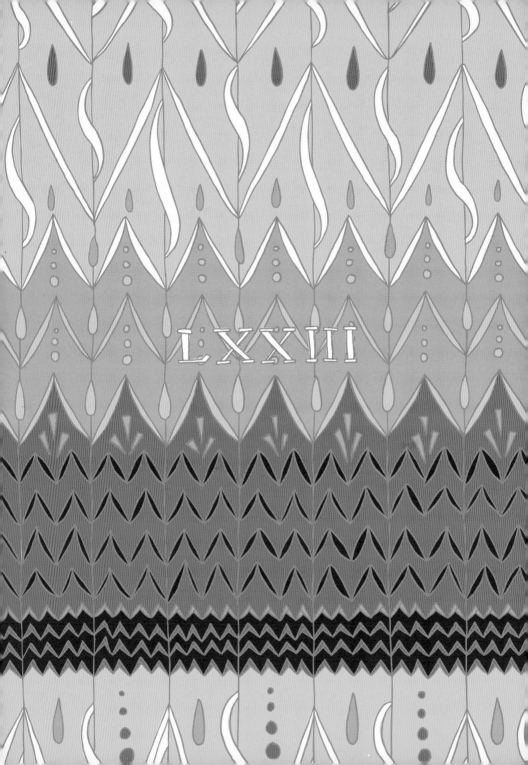

LXXIII

That time of year thou mayst in me behold

When yellow leaves, or none, or few, do hang

Upon those boughs which shake against the cold,

Bare ruin'd choirs, where late the sweet birds sang.

In me thou see'st the twilight of such day

As after sunset fadeth in the west;

Which by and by black night doth take away,

Death's second self, that seals up all in rest.

In me thou see'st the glowing of such fire,

That on the ashes of his youth doth lie,

As the death-bed, whereon it must expire,

Consum'd with that which it was nourish'd by.

This thou perceiv'st, which makes thy love more strong,

To love that well which thou must leave ere long.

XCVI

Some say thy grace is youth and gentle sport;

Both grace and faults are lov'd of more and less:

Thou mak'st faults graces that to thee resort.

As on the finger of a throned queen

The basest jewel will be well esteem'd,

So are those errors that in thee are seen

To truths translated and for true things deem'd.

How many lambs might the stern wolf betray,

If like a lamb he could his looks translate!

How many gazers mightst thou lead away,

If thou wouldst use the strength of all thy state!

But do not so; I love thee in such sort,

As, thou being mine, mine is thy good report.

XCVII

How like a winter hath my absence been
From thee, the pleasure of the fleeting year!
What freezings have I felt, what dark days seen!
What old December's bareness everywhere!
And yet this time removed was summer's time;
The teeming autumn, big with rich increase,
Bearing the wanton burden of the prime,
Like widow'd wombs after their lords' decease:
Yet this abundant issue seem'd to me
But hope of orphans and unfather'd fruit;
For summer and his pleasures wait on thee,
And, thou away, the very birds are mute:
Or, if they sing, 'tis with so dull a cheer,
That leaves look pale, dreading the winter's near.

XCVIII

From you have I been absent in the spring,
When proud-pied April, dress'd in all his trim,
Hath put a spirit of youth in every thing,
That heavy Saturn laugh'd and leap'd with him.
Yet nor the lays of birds nor the sweet smell
Of different flowers in odour and in hue,
Could make me any summer's story tell,
Or from their proud lap pluck them where they grew:
Nor did I wonder at the lily's white,
Nor praise the deep vermilion in the rose;
They were but sweet, but figures of delight,
Drawn after you, you pattern of all those.
Yet seem'd it winter still, and you away,
As with your shadow I with these did play.

XCIX

The forward violet thus did I chide:

Sweet thief, whence didst thou steal thy sweet that smells,

If not from my love's breath? The purple pride

Which on thy soft cheek for complexion dwells

In my love's veins thou hast too grossly dy'd.

The lily I condemned for thy hand,

And buds of marjoram had stol'n thy hair;

The roses fearfully on thorns did stand,

One blushing shame, another white despair;

A third, nor red nor white, had stol'n of both,

And to his robbery had annex'd thy breath;

But, for his theft, in pride of all his growth

A vengeful canker eat him up to death.

More flowers I noted, yet I none could see,

But sweet, or colour it had stol'n from thee.

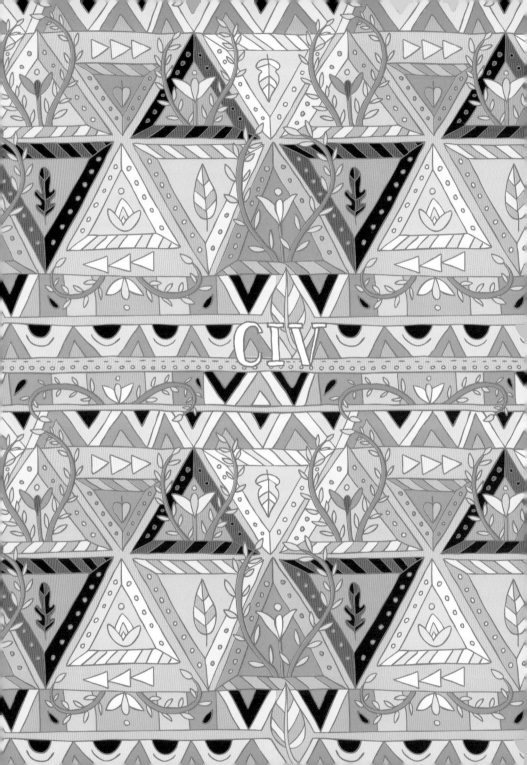
CIV

To me, fair friend, you never can be old,

For as you were when first your eye I eyed,

Such seems your beauty still. Three winters cold,

Have from the forests shook three summers' pride,

Three beauteous springs to yellow autumn turn'd,

In process of the seasons have I seen,

Three April perfumes in three hot Junes burn'd,

Since first I saw you fresh, which yet are green.

Ah! yet doth beauty like a dial-hand,

Steal from his figure, and no pace perceiv'd;

So your sweet hue, which methinks still doth stand,

Hath motion, and mine eye may be deceiv'd:

For fear of which, hear this thou age unbred:

Ere you were born was beauty's summer dead.

et not my love be call'd idolatry,

Nor my beloved as an idol show,

Since all alike my songs and praises be

To one, of one, still such, and ever so.

Kind is my love to-day, to-morrow kind,

Still constant in a wondrous excellence;

Therefore my verse to constancy confin'd,

One thing expressing, leaves out difference.

'Fair, kind, and true,' is all my argument,

'Fair, kind, and true,' varying to other words;

And in this change is my invention spent,

Three themes in one, which wondrous scope affords.

Fair, kind, and true, have often liv'd alone,

Which three till now, never kept seat in one.

When in the chronicle of wasted time

I see descriptions of the fairest wights,

And beauty making beautiful old rhyme,

In praise of ladies dead and lovely knights,

Then, in the blazon of sweet beauty's best,

Of hand, of foot, of lip, of eye, of brow,

I see their antique pen would have express'd

Even such a beauty as you master now.

So all their praises are but prophecies

Of this our time, all you prefiguring;

And for they looked but with divining eyes,

They had not skill enough your worth to sing:

For we, which now behold these present days,

Had eyes to wonder, but lack tongues to praise.

ot mine own fears, nor the prophetic soul

Of the wide world dreaming on things to come,

Can yet the lease of my true love control,

Supposed as forfeit to a confin'd doom.

The mortal moon hath her eclipse endur'd,

And the sad augurs mock their own presage;

Incertainties now crown themselves assur'd,

And peace proclaims olives of endless age.

Now with the drops of this most balmy time,

My love looks fresh, and Death to me subscribes,

Since, spite of him, I'll live in this poor rhyme,

While he insults o'er dull and speechless tribes:

And thou in this shalt find thy monument,

When tyrants' crests and tombs of brass are spent.

CIX

O! never say that I was false of heart,

Though absence seem'd my flame to qualify,

As easy might I from my self depart

As from my soul which in thy breast doth lie:

That is my home of love: if I have rang'd,

Like him that travels, I return again;

Just to the time, not with the time exchang'd,

So that myself bring water for my stain.

Never believe though in my nature reign'd,

All frailties that besiege all kinds of blood,

That it could so preposterously be stain'd,

To leave for nothing all thy sum of good;

For nothing this wide universe I call,

Save thou, my rose, in it thou art my all.

CXVI

et me not to the marriage of true minds

Admit impediments. Love is not love

Which alters when it alteration finds,

Or bends with the remover to remove:

O, no! it is an ever-fixed mark,

That looks on tempests and is never shaken;

It is the star to every wandering bark,

Whose worth's unknown, although his height be taken.

Love's not Time's fool, though rosy lips and cheeks

Within his bending sickle's compass come;

Love alters not with his brief hours and weeks,

But bears it out even to the edge of doom.

If this be error and upon me prov'd,

I never writ, nor no man ever lov'd.

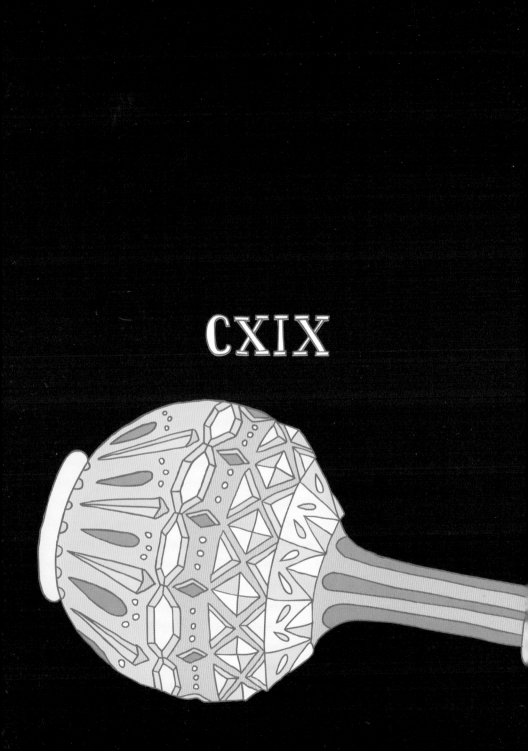

CXIX

hat potions have I drunk of Siren tears,

Distill'd from limbecks foul as hell within,

Applying fears to hopes, and hopes to fears,

Still losing when I saw myself to win!

What wretched errors hath my heart committed,

Whilst it hath thought itself so blessed never!

How have mine eyes out of their spheres been fitted,

In the distraction of this madding fever!

O benefit of ill! now I find true

That better is, by evil still made better;

And ruin'd love, when it is built anew,

Grows fairer than at first, more strong, far greater.

So I return rebuk'd to my content,

And gain by ill thrice more than I have spent.

CXXVIII

ow oft, when thou, my music, music play'st,

Upon that blessed wood whose motion sounds

With thy sweet fingers, when thou gently sway'st

The wiry concord that mine ear confounds,

Do I envy those jacks that nimble leap,

To kiss the tender inward of thy hand,

Whilst my poor lips, which should that harvest reap,

At the wood's boldness by thee blushing stand!

To be so tickled, they would change their state

And situation with those dancing chips,

O'er whom thy fingers walk with gentle gait,

Making dead wood more bless'd than living lips.

Since saucy jacks so happy are in this,

Give them thy fingers, me thy lips to kiss.

CXXX

My mistress' eyes are nothing like the sun;

Coral is far more red, than her lips red;

If snow be white, why then her breasts are dun;

If hairs be wires, black wires grow on her head.

I have seen roses damask'd, red and white,

But no such roses see I in her cheeks;

And in some perfumes is there more delight

Than in the breath that from my mistress reeks.

I love to hear her speak, yet well I know

That music hath a far more pleasing sound:

I grant I never saw a goddess go;

My mistress, when she walks, treads on the ground:

And yet by heaven, I think my love as rare,

As any she belied with false compare.

When my love swears that she is made of truth,

I do believe her though I know she lies,

That she might think me some untutor'd youth,

Unlearned in the world's false subtleties.

Thus vainly thinking that she thinks me young,

Although she knows my days are past the best,

Simply I credit her false speaking tongue:

On both sides thus is simple truth suppress'd:

But wherefore says she not she is unjust?

And wherefore say not I that I am old?

O! love's best habit is in seeming trust,

And age in love, loves not to have years told:

Therefore I lie with her, and she with me,

And in our faults by lies we flatter'd be.

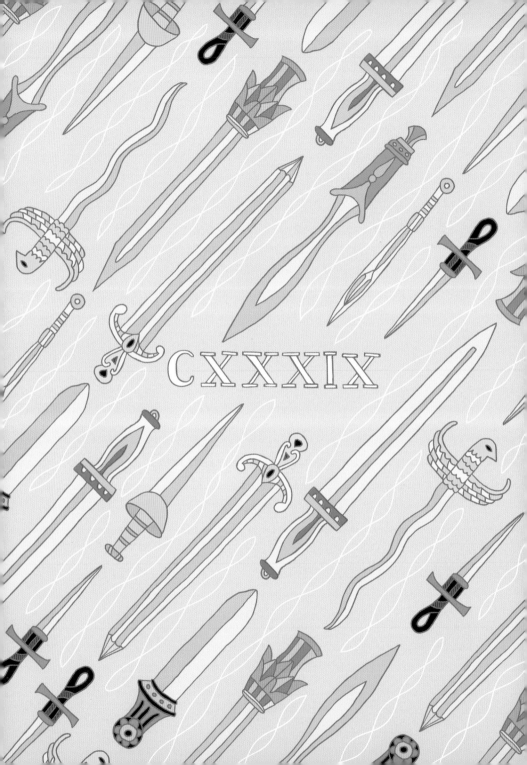

CXXXIX

O! call not me to justify the wrong

That thy unkindness lays upon my heart;

Wound me not with thine eye but with thy tongue:

Use power with power and slay me not by art.

Tell me thou lov'st elsewhere; but in my sight,

Dear heart, forbear to glance thine eye aside:

What need'st thou wound with cunning, when thy might

Is more than my o'er-press'd defense can bide?

Let me excuse thee: ah! my love well knows

Her pretty looks have been mine enemies;

And therefore from my face she turns my foes,

That they elsewhere might dart their injuries:

Yet do not so; but since I am near slain,

Kill me outright with looks and rid my pain.

CLIII

Cupid laid by his brand and fell asleep;

A maid of Dian's this advantage found,
And his love-kindling fire did quickly steep
In a cold valley-fountain of that ground;
Which borrow'd from this holy fire of Love,
A dateless lively heat, still to endure,
And grew a seething bath, which yet men prove
Against strange maladies a sovereign cure.
But at my mistress' eye Love's brand new-fired,
The boy for trial needs would touch my breast;
I, sick withal, the help of bath desired,
And thither hied, a sad distemper'd guest,
But found no cure, the bath for my help lies
Where Cupid got new fire; my mistress' eyes.

Caitlin Keegan is an illustrator and designer whose work
has been featured in *Bust*, the *New York Times*, *Nylon*, and
other publications. She lives in Brooklyn.

Library of Congress Cataloging-in-Publication
Data available.

ISBN: 978-0-8118-7908-8

Sonnets selected by Deborah Willis, Professor of
English, University of California, Riverside

Manufactured in China.

10 9 8 7 6 5 4 3 2 1

Chronicle Books LLC
680 Second Street
San Francisco, CA 94107
www.chroniclebooks.com

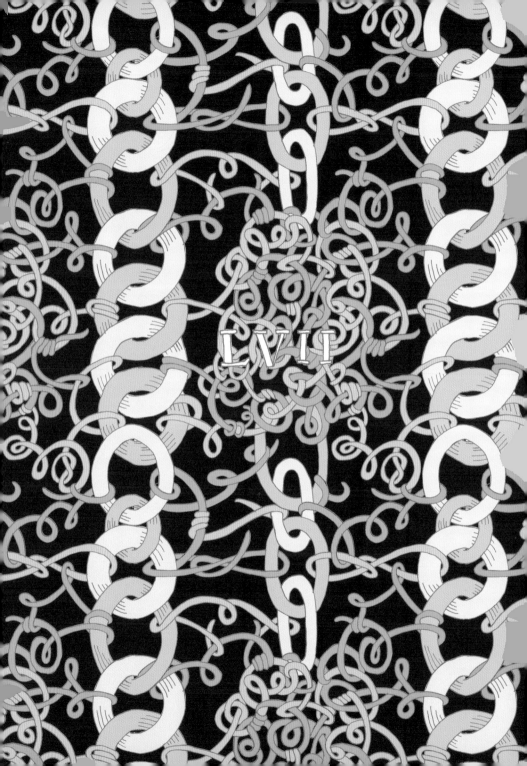

LVII